Future Employment of Power: Strategic Inferences for India

Future Employment of Air Power: Strategic Inferences for India

Air Marshal (Dr) Diptendu Choudhury,
PVSM, AVSM, VM, VSM (Retd)

United Service Institution of India
New Delhi (India)

Vij Books
New Delhi (India)

Published by

Vij Books
(Publishers, Distributors & Importers)
4836/24, Ansari Road
Delhi – 110 002
Phones: 91-11-43596460
Mob: 98110 94883
e-mail: contact@vijpublishing.com
web : www.vijbooks.in

First Published in India in 2025

Copyright © 2025, United Service Institution of India, New Delhi

ISBN: 978-81-98063-69-4

All rights reserved.

No part of this book may be reproduced, stored in a retrieval system, transmitted or utilized in any form or by any means, electronic, mechanical, photocopying, recording or otherwise, without the prior permission of the copyright owner. Application for such permission should be addressed to the publisher.

The views expressed in this monograph are of the author/authors in his/their personal capacity and do not represent the views of the USI.

Contents

Introduction		1
Chapter 1	Control of the Air: An Enduring Criticality	5
Chapter 2	The Expanding Offensive Air Power	10
Chapter 3	The Fusion of Strategic Air Operations and Offensive Air Defence	15
Chapter 4	The Future of Airspace Management	20
Chapter 5	An Integrated Aerospace Domain Awareness Capability	25
Chapter 6	From Integrated Air Defence to Integrated Aerospace Defence	29
Chapter 7	Future Generation Fighters	32
Chapter 8	Aerospace Technology and Production Capability	37
Conclusion		41
Endnotes		44

Introduction

Recent and ongoing conflicts reflect the evolving nature of warfare, particularly in how new paradigms of air power employment are continuously emerging alongside advances in aviation-related technology. The notion of a 'Reducing appetite for wars' among nations has proved transient, as shifting geopolitics, transitional polarity, and national interests ensure that the use of force remains a viable instrument for both state and non-state entities. The nature of war has transformed, with an increase in the types of conflicts, the number of participants, and the duration of engagements, while the scale of death, destruction, and damage inflicted has multiplied. The blurred lines between conventional, hybrid, grey zone and the no-war-no-peace conflicts resonate with the quote by the two People's Liberation Army Air Force (PLAAF) Colonels, "The war Gods face has become indistinct".[1] Although the original context discusses technology rendering the contemporary battlefield less distinct, it aptly reflects the erosion of the erstwhile norm of formally declaring war. It appears that the national interests of a state or a coalition of states now take precedence over historical norms, negating the need for formal declarations of conflict. Of greater concern is that wars and conflicts are no longer the exclusive domain of states; they have become open territory for non-state actors and entities. This shift has placed an enormous burden on global militaries, requiring them to plan, prepare, equip, and train for a vastly expanded spectrum of force employment.

One fact evident since the turn of the century is that the exploitation of the aerial domain and the leveraging of air power in contemporary conflicts have not only increased; if anything, its rapid adaptation of technology, tailored to conflict dynamics, has made it a *sine qua non* of modern warfare. Whether it is Russia's extensive conventional kinetic employment in the Ukraine war, Israel's aerial pounding of Gaza, Myanmar's military air strikes against anti-junta resistance, or the innovative Houthi rebels disrupting Red Sea traffic with drone and missile attacks, which invited retaliatory air strikes by the United States (US) and Allied Forces, or the recent Turkish air strikes against Kurdish militants in Syria and Iraq, the list continues to grow. At the other end of the spectrum, the use of air power for coercion and political signalling remains significant in all major and potential conflict zones. China's aggressive and escalating use of the PLAAF with the employment of large mixed formations of fighters, bombers, and Airborne Early Warning and Control (AEWC) aircraft, to transgress Taiwan's airspace has in effect erased the sanctity of the Median Line in the Strait separating the two nations.[2]

Contemporary conflicts and future geopolitical outlooks emphasise the continued salience of air power in a nation's security strategies, national interests, and joint military strategies. Air forces must continuously adapt to and adopt rapidly changing technologies to keep their tactics, concepts of operations, and warfighting strategies future-relevant, which inherently necessitates regular doctrinal reviews. The Indian Air Force's (IAF's) latest doctrine hence covers its doctrinal and structural engagement with the nations' joint military strategy, as well as the land and maritime strategies, across the entire spectrum and levels of conflict.[3] At the same time, the IAF, and indeed the other services, must remain constantly aware that training requirements for each type of conflict across the spectrum are not universal. While engaged with the specifics of one type of conflict, they must ensure that the skills necessary for other types are not lost. The air power capabilities of a nation's air force must be prepared for employment across the entire spectrum of conflict. It must remain agile and flexible to absorb ongoing changes in air warfare and be proficient in adopting best-proven practices worldwide. The challenge in current conflicts is that, amidst all the associated white noise of their circumstances and conduct, clear outcomes that align with the aims and goals of the respective protagonists are yet to emerge. Understanding the context of each conflict is important, as there will be commonalities and differences amongst them, and therefore, lessons or takeaways will also have common threads, vast differences, and contradictions.[4]

India's future conflicts cannot assuredly be confined to escalation-controlled border skirmishes. There is a high probability that its wars will be conventional, prolonged, and crucial to its future regional geopolitical dynamics and international power status. Today, a 'Joint approach in India's continental threat calculus is no longer seen as a binary between the two armies, but hearteningly as one multi-domain threat with a joint military strategy. The serious initiatives being taken towards establishing a joint military approach for the future employment of force in India's national security are indicative that the military leadership is already seized of its dire necessity'. The critical imperative of the continental threat is a national security priority and has to be dealt with by India on its own, essentially by the army and the air force.[5] In the end, given the clear and present immediate continental security concerns, the need for strengthening the nations' offensive airpower and Air Defence (AD) capabilities is a joint multi-domain imperative for the long-term strengthening of the conventional deterrence capability of India's military instrument.[6]

Closer to home, air power remains a critical factor in the real and present danger posed by India's continental threat from two nuclear-armed adversaries with formidable air forces, who share a close strategic alliance. Given that India's threat spectrum spans the nuclear and conventional to the more diffused hybrid and grey zone threats, there are significant strategic and tactical air power-related insights to be drawn from contemporary battlefields and conflict zones, impacting our current and future national security and military strategy. This monograph focuses on key strategic aspects of air power relevant to India's future security context.

CHAPTER 1

Control of the Air: An Enduring Criticality

"In the employment of air power in conflict situations, there is one area that is relatively easy to predict for the future – irrespective of any other demands that will be placed on air power, it will be primarily tasked to obtain and maintain control of the air, across the entire spectrum of conflict".

- *Sanu Kainikara, 2016[7]*

From a conventional war perspective, Russia's employment of air power in the Russo-Ukraine War has highlighted structural, doctrinal, and organisational shortcomings in its military strategy. The Cold War-centric legacy approach to the defensive employment of air power within contemporary military strategy has resulted in its sub-optimal utilisation. Unlike the American and that of most modern militaries, the Russian military strategy does not allow its air force or the *Vozdushno-kosmicheskiye sily* (Aerospace Forces [VKS]) the freedom to pursue an air campaign. It also doctrinally does not require the air force to offensively seize control of the adversarial air space and facilitate the surface campaign.[8] Thus, Russia's air power employment is limited to utilisation in tactical support of the ground campaign and the AD of the *Rodina*, or the motherland. The shortcomings of this suboptimal employment of its significant air power capability have been evident in the ongoing war with Ukraine.

The absence of a counter-air strategy, insufficient follow-through on the initial coordinated air and missile strikes, and an inadequately executed Suppression of Enemy Air Defence (SEAD) campaign led to the failure to gain control over Ukrainian airspace. This not only costed Russia the initiative in the air campaign but also stalled its surface campaign at the war's outset, as the small yet vastly outnumbered Ukrainian air force, or *Povitryani syly Zbroynykh syl Ukrayiny* (air force of the armed forces of Ukraine [PS ZSU]), effectively restricted the VKS's air operations during the initial days, inflicting significant losses. The ineffective SEAD campaign allowed the PS ZSU to regroup its AD assets, and with extensive support from the North Atlantic Treaty Organisation (NATO) was initially able to deny the VKS the freedom to operate over Ukrainian airspace. Thus, their effort to carry out swift offensive operations by employing precepts of mass and manoeuvre, without achieving a viable degree of control of air, has consequently led to greater Russian Army and air force losses. According to David Deptula–"Russia has never fully appreciated the use of airpower beyond support to ground forces. As a result, Russia, in all its wars, has never conceived of or run a strategic air campaign".[9] Thus, despite having a powerful air force, the inability of a nation to leverage the aerial domain by exploiting this potent military instrument to the fullest of its capabilities to achieve military objectives and national aims is possibly the most significant lesson of contemporary modern wars.

In the sub-conventional conflict realm, where there is no air opposition from the adversary, control of air allows unfettered employment of air power over the conflict spaces and the option of providing kinetic support without committing boots on the ground. 'The US military and its coalition partners—29 countries that contributed military support—instead played a supporting role, primarily contributing critical airpower to combat operations against the Islamic State of Iraq and Syria (ISIS). For example, airpower halted ISIS's 2014 offensive, notably saving Baghdad, Erbil, and Kobani. Strategic air strikes then weakened ISIS finances by targeting the group›s cash reserves and oil business. Iraqi and Syrian partners would not have been able to retake territory from ISIS without coalition airpower, which provided essential intelligence and precision strikes and bolstered partner troops' confidence and motivation against a fearsome enemy'.[10] In fact, the introduction of Russian airpower in Syria has been widely cited as a turning point in the Syrian civil war, as it played a decisive role in reversing the fortunes of the Syrian regime. Russia's intervention was designed as a limited-liability expeditionary campaign, with a small theatre footprint predicated on Russian air and naval power supporting regime ground forces.[11] Offensive employment of air power against non-state entities like Hamas and Hezbollah by Israel and by the US and the United Kingdom (UK) against the Houthi Rebels are more recent examples. The caveat is that, while these entities may lack conventional air power assets, they certainly possess access to affordable, low-technology options in anti-aircraft capabilities, such as surface-to-air missiles, alongside offensive capabilities in the form of surface-launched rockets, long-range missiles, and drones.

In the Indian context, with two strong opposing air forces, all future battlespaces will be highly contested. China and Pakistan will exploit the aerial dimension offensively to further their military objectives. Aside from future use of manned and unmanned platforms, long-range surface and space-launched vectors will definitively be used offensively to strike deep into Indian Territory to target military, industry and strategic assets and infrastructure, in addition to air operations over the tactical battle spaces. Thus, some degree of control of air will be mandatory for joint operations, as enemy will seek to use its air power offensively to disrupt surface operations. In current circumstances, while air superiority is extremely unlikely in highly contested spaces, favourable air situations for defined periods over designated tactical spaces will be possible and remain a critical requirement for the IAF, not just for air operations but especially so for all joint operations.

The salience of control of the air has yet again been underscored in contemporary conventional wars. The degree of the control of air will, however, depend on the air power capability of the adversary. The absence of any air opposition where the adversary has no AD capability will lead to benign air spaces, and in case of a limited adversarial AD capability, it will lead to low-threat air spaces. When fighting an enemy with an air force, the size and capability of the adversarial air power will dictate the quantum of air opposition and the degree of control of air possible. Fighting against an adversary with a small air force or a limited air power capability will involve contested air spaces of relatively low intensity, where a significant degree of control of air can be achieved.

In the present and the foreseeable future, wars or conflicts against adversaries with strong air forces will involve highly contested air spaces, where any degree of control of the air will have to be fought for. In India's case, as both adversaries possess strong air forces, control of the air will need to be secured from the adversary across tactical battlespaces, penetration corridors, and hostile airspaces to conduct all joint operations, offensive air strikes, and strategic targeting in depth. This control, however, will be transient and limited to designated spaces and periods. Thus, control of air is no longer an air force-only requirement but a critical joint warfighting necessity, especially in India's continental threat scenario. Therefore, it must be integral to the nation's joint military strategy.

Air power remains a vital instrument of a nation's military power, as is evident in all contemporary conflicts. Combined with the salience of the aerial domain, which offers overarching vertical envelopment over land and sea, it represents a critical multi-domain warfighting capability essential for the future. Thus, India can no longer look at its national security from the exclusive continental and maritime domain perspectives. Instead, it must integrate air and space power comprehensively with land and sea powers to adopt a multi-domain approach in the nation's military strategy and national security outlook.

Chapter 2

The Expanding Offensive Air Power

"Offensive air power is thus a future military necessity, whether used collaboratively in the continental or maritime realms, or as an independent hard power instrument in the wider national interest".[12]

Fighter and bomber aircraft have been the traditional aerial weapon delivery platforms for the offensive application of air power. While they will remain the mainstay instruments for deep strikes, the proliferation of advanced area denial AD systems and a wide range of tactical surface-to-air missile systems have raised the vulnerability of all aerial platforms. Thus, stand-off targeting and long-range air-launched weapons that can be launched from outside the AD threat envelope have become increasingly relevant for aerial weapon delivery. To mitigate the increased AD threat in hostile air spaces, advances in self-protection suites of aerial delivery platforms are also evolving rapidly to enable manned and unmanned platforms to penetrate enemy area denial and AD systems. Modern and future manned platforms incorporate design features that include tactical penetration aids employing electronic warfare, low observable platform and sensor technology, active and passive countermeasures, advanced threat warning and dispensing systems, self-protection suites, and decoys. Unlike expendable single-use drones, future reusable unmanned platforms, which are expected to operate in tactical battlespaces and inside enemy AD coverage, will also incorporate a modicum of self-protection to survive in hostile airspaces.

The only alternatives to manned platforms for carrying deep strikes inside the enemy heartland are air and surface-launched cruise missiles and long-range advanced drones. Typically, long-range missiles and stand-off targeting have limitations in accuracy, weapon-to-target matching, and the over-the-target throw weight needed to achieve the necessary effects, among other factors. The enormous quantity of rockets, cruise, and hypersonic missiles employed has not yielded the desired war outcomes for Russia, primarily due to two key factors: weapon accuracy and weight of attack. The first factor necessitates advanced delivery systems and seeker heads, which come at a high cost; thus, increased accuracy correlates with increased expense. The second factor is that to achieve a greater weight of attack, more weapons will need to be fired against a target to achieve the desired level of destruction. Again, a higher quantum of weapons used will entail correspondingly lower cost-effectiveness. Therefore, cost-effectiveness becomes an issue with expensive modern weapons vis-à-vis the selected target systems being attacked, and their future development will depend on the value of the target system, the quantum of such a threat, and the ability of a military to afford the possession of such weapons in the numbers desired.[13] In the Indian context, with two major nuclear-armed threats to contend with, the extensive hostile borders and the vast volume of airspace involved present a scale of threat unparalleled elsewhere in the world. This necessity versus affordability in adequate numbers of all expensive weapon systems will always remain a challenge for the budget-constrained Indian military.

The high and medium-altitude Intelligence, Surveillance, and Reconnaissance (ISR) drones that gained credibility in precision targeting in the US global war on terror, are extremely vulnerable to advanced AD systems, due to their low speeds and limited manoeuvrability. The simple fact is that the most advanced contemporary drones like the US MQ 9 Reaper, the Chinese Wing Loong II, Turkish Bayraktar TB 2, etc., are all extremely vulnerable to enemy AD in contested and highly contested air spaces. The development of advanced drones that operationally complement fighter jets, relying on direct control of their manned peers or on-board AI, is being developed as the Manned-Unmanned Teaming (MUMT) concept. It can scout the battlefield, engage the enemy and sacrifice itself to shield manned aircraft. The US Valkyrie XQ 58A and the Sukhoi S 70 are expected to provide cost-effective unmanned team solutions. Being almost as capable as manned fighters in specific roles, but with the advantage of being cheap and easily replaceable allows large numbers of the type to saturate enemy defences.[14] On the other end of the drone spectrum, while small drones have delivered some successes in tactical battle areas, they have not produced strategic outcomes in the ongoing wars. The Royal United Service Institute estimates that Ukraine has lost approximately 10,000 drones monthly, indicating their widespread use and high loss rate.[15] Drone employment in conflicts and warfare has proliferated as they have made their place in all the warfighting domains, of air, land and sea. However, they are not an end in themselves when it comes to the means of prosecuting aerial warfare, and they are certainly not the game-changer as the much-vested drone industry makes them out to be.

On the other hand, while the vulnerability of manned fighters has increased as well, they will continue to remain relevant in both defensive and offensive avatars because of their flexibility and wide range of applications, the cost-effectiveness of their multiple reusability as a launch platform, advantage of targeting discrimination, multi-role-multi-task and multi-mission capability, future manned-unmanned teaming options, etc. The continued investment of all major powers in strengthening their air forces and continued hectic-paced research and development in future warfare-focussed advances in new-generation fighters tell their own story of the ever-growing relevance of offensive air power. What is certain in India's future wars is that the border-centric offensive/defensive operations on their own will not be able to produce the desired warfighting outcomes without the conduct of depth and strategic targeting to carry the fury and the will of the nation deep into the enemy's heartland. Here the role of the entire expanded range of air power's offensive capabilities will come into play. Thus, the future offensive air power capabilities that have expanded rapidly from the erstwhile exclusivity of manned platform to include manned-unmanned teams, advanced hypersonic missiles, cruise missiles, a wide range of drones, advanced long-range stand-off air and surface launched weapons, etc., irrespective of service specific ownership, will become integral to the military's joint application of offensive power.

Offensive air power is no longer exclusive to bombers and fighter aircraft. The contemporary and the future will include a wide range of manned and unmanned combat and weapon delivery platforms, as well as an increasing range of weaponry, whether launched from air, land, sea or space, which will use the vertical domain domains of air and space for launch or transit. The future construct of India's offensive air power must include the entire range of offensive capabilities of aviation assets and surface-launched long-range weapons to enable a joint application of force for joint military outcomes.

The major air forces all over the world are already adapting to the future requirements of unmanned systems, as all leading nations or groups of nations are investing in the advanced generation of manned and unmanned platforms, and associated technologies. IAF's current offensive capability provides a degree of asymmetric air power advantage vis-à-vis the Pakistan Air Force (PAF) and the PLAAF. While Indian air power will remain dominant over the PAF in the foreseeable future, albeit with a reducing force-ratio advantage, the margin of asymmetric advantage which the IAF currently enjoys due to geography and deployed force ratios with respect to the PLAAF, however, will tilt the balance in favour of the latter very soon. A collusive air power threat will put the IAF on the defensive to the detriment of all surface and joint operations, in all future wars, conflicts, or operations. The reality of a growing collusive air power threat is a serious future concern, given the extensive air power engagements and air exercises between the PLAAF and the PAF.

The frenetic pace of the development and expansion of China's air power capability in the Tibet Autonomous Region post-Galwan is a tacit acceptance of the necessity to alter the air power asymmetry in its favour. This will be a strategic vulnerability as it will effectively neutralise the only depth offensive and conventional deterrence advantage that India currently enjoys against China. New Delhi needs to recognise and accept the criticality and long-term strategic consequences of this reality to India's military and national security. It must do all it can to prevent the reversal of the current asymmetric air power advantage to the detriment of India's future continental security, with the timely prioritisation of the nation's future air power requirements.

CHAPTER 3

The Fusion of Strategic Air Operations and Offensive Air Defence

"As it is, the ground forces across the world have traditionally found it much more difficult to understand the role of military beyond the immediate experience and context of the land battle and the immediate effects of applied force. But a major proportion of the role of air power and its impact takes place beyond the immediate battle on the ground and the visual range of the troops".

- Jasjit Singh, 2013[16]

Strategic targeting and offensive strikes/interdiction deep inside the enemy territory are the primary roles of the IAF. It is only the Air Force's offensive capabilities that can engage depth targets of strategic and economic importance e.g., vital industries and production facilities, oil facilities, power systems, distribution grids, road-rail communication networks, ports, bridges, military assets and infrastructure, etc. This role is critical to the nation's military capability and warfighting strategy, as air power carries the war deep into the enemy's territory and consciousness. Depth offensive by the IAF is vital to all surface operations as it has a direct impact on the Indian Army's (IA) Tactical Battle Areas (TBAs) as strategic air operations and interdiction operations target the enemy's reserves, fuel, power, command and communication nodes, supply and logistics, etc., in depth and deny/degrade their access to the battlespaces. Without strategic offensive capability, the ability of the IA to sustain its operations given the logistic combat supply-chain and connectivity disparity, especially against China, would be critically affected. Surface to surface missile forces will certainly complement this capability in the future, but can never replace the sheer quantum, scale, wide range of bespoke targeting options, and operational flexibility that the IAF brings to the table of the nations offensive capability.

Russia's extensive targeting of Ukraine's 'Electric power industry is part of the energy sector that has suffered the greatest damage since the Russian invasion in 2022, estimated in Jun to top USD 11.4 bn, with three-quarters of the losses in generation facilities and the remainder in networks' and early estimates of build back costs are estimated around USD 30 bn.[17] Russia's 'Bombing campaign has succeeded in destroying multiple power plants, damaging a gas storage site, and disabling electricity transmission infrastructure across Ukraine' and the recent escalation of the air war has led to a 'Number of Ukraine's hydroelectric power plants been targeted in the latest wave of attacks. This raise concerns over a potential ecological disaster if dams on some of Ukraine's biggest waterways are breached'.[18] It is Russia's strategic targeting that has taken the war to the people of Ukraine as the battles rage in the tactical battle spaces. Future warfighting cannot be expected to remain limited to contact battle on the frontlines and produce war outcomes. Thus, offensive targeting in depth will remain a major role of offensive air power, simply because surface-launched rocket/missile forces have their limits of size, range, throw-weight, accuracy and numbers. Air power will continue to do the major share of offensive depth targeting in the foreseeable future in the Indian context as well.

The Fusion of Strategic Air Operations and Offensive Air Defence

The short-lived fight for survival by the small Ukrainian air force was an operational inevitability against the powerful Russian air force. In the absence of long-range beyond visual range missiles, inadequate ground radar cover and extensive threat envelope of Russian Surface-to-Air Guided Weapon (SAGW) systems, its 'Battle of Britain' moment failed to turn the tide. Despite significant initial losses and in the absence of a contemporary air power application strategy, the Russian air force is continuing its business as usual. The much-vaunted concept of the 'Air Denial' concept has not been able to significantly impact Russian air power, which merely resorted to a change in tactics to stay out of the NATO-assisted lethal mobile AD network and resort to extensive stand-off aerial targeting. Air denial is resorted to by a nation with a weak or non-existent air force, and is a defensive concept. It is not an air power strategy, but an operational expediency of nations with weak air forces. While a robust AD is a warfighting necessity, it cannot compensate for the lack of the offensive capability of modern air power. The IAF ranks third in Global Air Power ranking after the US and Russian air powers, based not on overall strength but on modernisation, logistical support, offensive and defensive capabilities, etc.,[19] and has a proven combat record and immense experience in contemporary international exercises. India must fully leverage IAF's significant air power capability in its military strategy as a potent offensive instrument across domains. Not to do so will be a redux of the 1962 Indo-China war debacle.

Fusion of AD with depth offensive air operations is already an operational reality of all professional air forces worldwide. The IAF is no exception with its Integrated AD (IAD) capability that synergises all AD operations with practically all air operations including depth offensive air operations. AD is critical to IAF's strike operations as they create the tactical conditions to penetrate Chinese Anti-Area-

Access-Denial (A2/AD) defence systems in Tibet and defeat Pakistan's multi-layered robust AD network. The extent of the IAD sensor and ground-based AD weapon system cover that extends adversarial airspace is critical as it will impact both IAF and IA operations in the future. A multi-layered combination of high, medium and low-level radars and multi-tiered Surface-to-Air Missile (SAM) systems with long, medium, short, and close-in weapons systems which comprise an IAD needs to be bolstered with extensive long-range SAM systems, to enable offensive AD operations as deep inside enemy airspace as a possible. The best AD is provided with the ability to see and target the enemy air deep inside the enemy airspace.

A potent Extended Integrated AD (EIAD) capability that synergises all sensors and weapons and provides an 'Offensive' AD capability deep inside the adversarial airspace is a strategic necessity for not just the IAF but indeed the IA as well, given its overarching criticality in all offensive and defensive operations. Extending the 'Sensor-shooter' reach with a potent EIAD capability across India's large continental spaces of varied terrain and environmental conditions is a vital national security requirement that is as much a wartime necessity as its peace-time imperative for AD of our sovereign airspace of the mainland and island territories.

EIAD serves as a counter to the enemy A2/AD as it enables friendly air power to penetrate deep inside the enemy's airspace for executing offensive strikes and AD operations. It is a future joint warfighting necessity as it will provide a much-needed asymmetry to offset the force ratio disadvantages faced by the IA in the northern contingency. Against Pakistan, with its strong AD system and air power, a potent Indian EIAD will serve to deny the enemy air force operational freedom and reduce the effectiveness of its offensive air operations against the IA. An EIAD capability deployed in the island territories on the east and west in the maritime domain will provide offensive AD cover over India's strategic areas of interest. A future-relevant EIAD capability and strategic offensive air power capability balance will play a definitive role in India's future multi-domain national security construct.

CHAPTER 4

The Future of Airspace Management

"The issue of ASM is even more important now with the range of users and variety of aerial platforms that have permeated the battle space".

- Gen MM Naravane (Retd)[20]

'Airspace Management' is a key aspect of air power employment and is often confused with 'Control of Air'. The latter pertains to the larger function of denying the enemy effective use of the vertical dimension over battlespaces and the airspace above enemy territory, which is a wartime function. Airspace management, on the other hand, is for the functional control to ensure the de-conflicted use of the sovereign airspace both in peace and war, to allow all friendly users access to it. During war, airspace management will also spill over to adversarial airspaces where active control of air exists. Modern battlespaces are intensely busy and dense volume of airspace which needs definite close surveillance and control, to ensure we can detect, identify and engage every air threat, and permit full freedom of operations for friendly aerial assets. Thus, airspace management is a complex responsibility of managing or controlling both sovereign airspace for all defensive AD operations, adversarial airspaces for AD of all offensive air operations, and AD operations over TBA. IAF's extended integrated AD system which includes airborne and ground-based sensors, as well as its multi-tiered SAGW systems and extended range beyond visual range equipped

AD fighters, operate in a sophisticated, well-integrated, and seamless networked manner to provide holistic AD cover across the entire range of IAF's air operations and IA's TBAs.

Future warfare will see a high density of aerial platforms operating in the airspaces over battle zones. In all leading military powers, air operations—fighters, transports, helicopters, remotely piloted aircraft, in peace and war, are strictly governed by airspace management norms. During hostilities, the entire volume of airspace, including the TBAs of the IA, will need to be closely managed to enable freedom of friendly air operations. The Indian airspace is where all air operations, including coordinated air missions, are conducted or transit through; it is where the ISR aircraft operate, where enemy air forces manoeuvre to support their operations and launch attacks, and, crucially, where all Indian artillery fire and long-range weapons also pass through. In recent conflicts, long-range rockets, cruise missiles, long-range missiles, stand-off weapons, and unmanned aerial systems have increased traffic density within tactical battle spaces. All IAF offensive missions are tightly integrated with Airborne Warning and Control System (AWACS), AEWC aircraft, and surface radar surveillance coverages, and are closely coordinated with all friendly AD, Combat Air Patrol (CAP) missions, and SAGW elements. Over and above these, every air movement is intricately coordinated and de-conflicted to ensure safe routing through the enemy's radar gaps, to enable protection by own AD aircraft and SAGW systems wherever possible and are kept secure from friendly weapon systems and firepower in the TBAs.[21]

TBAs of the future will typically comprise defined geographical spaces where the IA will be engaged in direct contact battle with the enemy. These will vary depending on the adversary, terrain, and military objectives, and depending on the type of surface operations, whether defensive or offensive, will require AD against the enemy's offensive air power. The freedom of IAF's AD operations over enemy airspaces and TBAs will be critical to all surface operations, given that both adversaries have strong air forces, which will seek to destroy, degrade, and deny the IA's fielded forces actively. Round the clock AD surveillance, control, reporting, assignation of SAGW systems and interceptors are conducted by the sector-wise AD nodes of the IAF. These not only provide 24x7 visibility of the entire Indian airspace and all future battlespaces but also involve trained specialist fighter controllers and battle managers on the ground and in the air, who closely control all offensive and AD operations. Threat detection of the enemy air and its engagement at maximum possible ranges, as well as the de-confliction, maximum exploitation, and fratricide prevention of all future air operations by the IAF and IA will only be possible with the automated and networked visibility of the entire volume of air space. This is only possible due to the Integrated Air Command and Control System (IACCS) which networks and data-links all surface and airborne radars and AD weapon systems. The IACCS is critical in ensuring the shortest possible sensor-shooter kill chain. The IA's AD requirements are comparatively much more limited in range and weapon envelopes and they fall well within the larger EIAD construct of the IAF. It would make enormous operational and tactical sense for the IA to integrate with the heavily invested and established extensive EIAD coverage, as it would enable a more comprehensive AD for all surface operations, whether defensive or offensive. This is why airspace management is and must remain an integral part of the AD function of the IAF, whether in peace or war.

Given India's enormous civil aviation industry and growth boom, the 'One Airspace' is a comprehensive program, projected to span over eight years, including infrastructure development, controller training, and migration to the new system. Once fully operational, the unified airspace strategy will enable airlines to identify more efficient flight routes and reduce travel time and fuel consumption. By facilitating consistent flight patterns at higher altitudes and smoother descents for landing, the initiative aims to enhance operational efficiency.[22] This is, however, only a civil aviation peacetime traffic management concept, which does not consider the wartime employment and management of sovereign airspace. The closure of airspace directly impacts the civil aviation industry and indirectly the economy, as did the disruption of civil air traffic over Pakistan due to the closure of air space post-Balakot cost it over INR 800 cr in revenue.[23] While IAF's operational airspace control ensured minimal disruption of civil air traffic, this will not be possible in an all-out war. The 'One Airspace' concept can only be for peacetime air management to enable greater seamless civil-military usage for day-to-day operations. Presently, a 'Flexible use of airspace' model is in place in India, which is aimed at greater integration of civil-military airspaces towards greater efficient use and aviation safety, through enhanced cooperation and coordination.[24] Wartime, however, will necessitate a future-relevant integration which warrants a holistic merge of all military and civil aviation to ensure total control of airspace on the invocation of the Union War Book. India's future sensor coverage must include all radars and future sensors, including space-based multi-spectral sensors. Integrating AD surveillance radars of the IA with the already integrated IAF and civil radar network architecture is a cost-effective and truly joint way forward. Active control over India's Air Defence Identification Zones (ADIZ)[25], must be factored into India's future architecture.

Future airspace control is vital as it maximises all air operations while ensuring AD coverage from enemy air, de-confliction with artillery fire and surface launched vectors, fratricide avoidance, de-conflicting friendly air traffic, collision avoidance, and finally enabling combat search and rescue.[26] Integration of advanced and common identification friend or foe of all aerial platforms with the future Integrated Aerospace Defence Architecture will ensure the safety of its aerial platforms while allowing full freedom of engagement of all types of adversarial aerial and space threats. War and peacetime airspace management protocols must be laid down and integrated into military strategy. All forms of aviation, military or civil will need to be under positive control and coordination in threat contingencies and war and must be exercised periodically.

A future relevant holistic integration of civil and military sovereign airspaces over India's mainland and island territories, which provides full freedom of application of military air power and maximises civil aviation operations during war and conflicts is way ahead. For this, the sensor coverage for the entire sovereign airspace, ADIZs, and the maritime spaces of interest need to be brought under the ambit of the Air Domain Awareness (ADA). Expanding India's aerial surveillance sensors over island territories is a future imperative given the strategic importance of the Indian Ocean Region (IOR) to India's economy, national security and vital interests. This is a future-relevant necessity to exercise positive control over the nation's sovereign air spaces and areas of interest over land and sea in peacetime and in war.

CHAPTER 5

An Integrated Aerospace Domain Awareness Capability

"Initially, the naval power was able to influence battles on land. Later, air power influenced war at land and seas. It is my belief that now, space will cast its influence on air, maritime and land domains".

- General Anil Chauhan[27]

For over a decade, extensive ADA already exists with the IAF's IACCS, which networks all IAF airborne and ground-based sensors together with AD shooters under regional AD Nodes to cover the mainland. In the long term, ADA would integrate all armed forces and civil aviation sensors. But will airspace management and control be enough in the future, given that at least near space will be extensively used for military applications? Will ADA be enough? While there is a welcome new realisation and drive towards greater ADA, it is not enough for the future. Most importantly, it needs to be upgraded conceptually to an 'Aerospace Domain Awareness', which includes the situational awareness of the air and near-space realms. Considering space has become a contested domain for competition and control that is increasingly being weaponised, India must move towards greater seamless awareness of the air, near-space and space domains. While situational awareness of outer space comes under space situational awareness and its extremely complex challenges, the need to monitor this domain along with the air and near-space domain below it is an undeniable future necessity. Thus, two areas of transformative paradigm transition and development are crucial for India's future. They are the development of an 'Integrated aerospace domain awareness capability' and the transition from an 'Integrated Air Defence' to an 'Integrated aerospace defence capability'.

China's extensive utilisation of space assets for A2/AD operations, encompassing both sea-based and land-based space programs for regional power projection, its sub-metric resolution satellite imaging capabilities, advanced space-based Command, Control, Communications, and Computers, ISR, as well as its expanding military capabilities reliant on space, are mounting concerns for India. Its space capabilities impact all aspects of conventional and nuclear targeting, ground-air-sea operations, precision conventional strike capacities, missile defence, direct-ascent and co-orbital ASAT weapons, directed-energy weapons, and cyber-ASAT capabilities[28] play a driving role in any future conflict with India. The current airspace situational awareness provided by the IAF's IACCS will not be enough as monitoring of India's sovereign aerospace, up to possibly the Karman line[29], will have to be integrated to be able to track all aerial vehicles, platforms and weapons in transit, which include ballistic missiles, long-range vectors, hypersonic glide vehicles, high altitude pseudo satellites, fractional orbital bombardment systems, and anti-satellite weapons. Thus, 'Airspace Control' has to expand its scope to 'Aerospace Control' in the future. For this, there is a fundamental necessity for a clear understanding of the vertical dimension and its critical salience of aerospace domain awareness of our sovereign spaces and areas of strategic and security interest.

Traditionally, India has been justifiably obsessed with its continental security, and very recently, the maritime domain has assumed great strategic significance. Two aspects stand out in India's isolated approach to the two surface domains which do not bode well for the future. The first is that the vertical domain of air has been seen from a very narrow and short-sighted perspective as an adjunct to the two domains, even though the aerial domain vertically envelopes and impacts both surface domains. The second aspect is that air and space mediums, while disparate in characteristics, are a continuum which has gained international ascendancy as a national security priority, given the rapidly increasing military exploitation by countries like the US, Russia and China. From a future national security context, the control of the nation's vertical aerospace domain is a necessity not just from a military perspective, but equally importantly from a civilian one, given the immense growth potential of India's civil aviation sector, and civil leveraging of space as a national enterprise. Fundamental to any aerospace control is the necessity of real-time three-dimensional multi-domain aerospace situational awareness. Given the differences between air and space domain characteristics, a fusion of awareness across both domains is an extremely challenging task but is a future-relevant necessity. However, the US Space Force comes under the Department of Air Force, the Russian Air Force has become the Russian Aerospace Force, and France has converted its air force to an air and space force. While the IAF has justifiably sought a change to an air and space force, this must not be construed as a claim to ownership of space. The IAF does not lay exclusive claim to space, considers it as national commons, and doctrinally clarifies that aerospace power is 'The sum of a nation's aerospace capabilities' and 'Includes the other services, civil aviation and space-related agencies which contribute to and leverage this multi-user domain of growing salience'.[30]

An Artificial Intelligence (AI)-enabled multi-domain integrated sensor fusion of air and space monitoring systems is the way ahead and must be prioritised as an area of research and development. Surface, aerial and space-based sensors, new generation aerial enabler platforms like the AEWC aircraft, AWACS platforms, future Joint Tactical Information Distribution System platforms, future ISR system platforms, future multi-sensor ISR systems, satellites, etc., must be integrated and networked to produce a three-dimensional aerospace combat situational awareness for India's national security.

India must accelerate its Research and Development (R&D) to create a comprehensive aerospace domain awareness architecture, which will need proactive handholding and synergy between India's space and aviation industry. The Department of Space Agency must drive this aggressively to enable greater air and space situational awareness of India's sovereign spaces and areas of interest.

The current combat-tested and proven IACCS of the IAF will have to be upgraded to an 'Integrated Aerospace Command and Control System' to serve as a golden thread which will network and weave all these elements into a cohesive and integrated system of systems.

Chapter 6

From Integrated Air Defence to Integrated Aerospace Defence

"With increasing use of space in military applications, it logically expands the term Airpower to Aerospace power with the need to defend and address the space-borne assets as well as their associated ground-based infrastructure".[31]

- Doctrine of the IAF

The barrage of firepower in future wars will not be limited to the battlespaces and will spill over into in-depth civilian spaces. Both of India's adversaries have strong air forces and the capability to target India's military, strategic, and civilian assets deep within the nation. Saturation air and missile strikes in India's high population-density rural and urban spaces resulting in mass civilian collateral are a reality that has not been given adequate attention. The important aspect to consider is that modern wars and conflicts will inevitably and unavoidably impact the civilian population as the fighting no longer remains limited to border battlespaces. The current conflict trends of mass-scale missile and rocket attacks against high-density population centres have expanded the employment options of the aerial dimension in warfare with their ability to carry the fight beyond the battlespaces, deeper into the adversary's heartland. They have also demonstrated their ability to bring the war to the doorsteps of a nation's citizens deep within rural and urban areas. Indian citizens are no strangers to terror attacks, and some sections of our border populations have experienced occasional firing and shelling, but a majority have no exposure to mass-scale conflict since the 1971 war.[32]

But keeping our population safe from enemy air attacks too has its limits, particularly considering India's geographical spread and population density. The state-of-the-art high-tech Iron Dome AD system has undoubtedly saved Israeli lives but has demonstrated that even the best of systems cannot assure a hundred per cent fail-safe AD. The sobering fact, however, is that despite the most modern AD systems, missiles, rockets, and drones will still manage to get through as no system can ensure total safety. This is especially relevant for India's national security, given the sheer geographical spread of over 7,000 km of hostile borders shared with China and Pakistan, and the humongous volume of sovereign airspace requiring AD coverage in war and peace. But is mere AD adequate for the future?

The current neo-realist national security outlook of the nation is a realpolitik-driven transition from the erstwhile approach of an exclusively civil-led peaceful use of space. China's military rise and the evident inclusion of space in its geopolitical strategy carry serious consequences for India. Its developments in future hypersonic weapons, space glide vehicles and fractional orbital bombardment systems, the ballistic missile early warning system, ASAT capabilities, including co-orbital systems, directed energy weapons, high-powered lasers, and space-enabled electronic jamming, spoofing, cyber means, etc., are a serious future threat and needs to be addressed on priority.[33]

IAF's responsibility for national AD has already expanded into the larger context of national aerospace defence for the future. The three-dimensional air situation awareness of air power has to concurrently transcend into a much-needed and future-relevant multi-domain aerospace awareness.[34]

In the future, as flight paths, orbital trajectories of aerial and space platforms, and long-range weapon trajectories increasingly utilise the near space for transit, AD needs to expand in its overall architecture to encompass both air and space, moving towards a more comprehensive 'Aerospace Defence' that holistically includes advanced AD, ballistic missile defence, and ASAT technology. It is high time India changed its current AD paradigms of the past to look at 'Aerospace Defence' holistically to include air and space, like the US, France, Russia, and China.

CHAPTER 7

Future Generation Fighters

"The PLAAF has invested heavily in developing multiple types of combat aircraft, including 5th Generation Fighter Aircraft".[35]

- Air Chief Marshal Arup Raha

Even as most air forces are struggling to upgrade their fighter inventories with 4.5 and 5th generation platforms, the 6th generation fighters are already under development by some nations on their own, and by some as a joint project. The US, Russia, China, and India are running their programs, while the UK, Italy, and Japan have a joint program, as have France, Germany and Spain. There are several commonalities in their platform designs, of which stealth and super-cruise are two important aspects. Advanced skin, airframe and engine designs are incorporated to reduce the sensor observability of the fighters across multiple spectrums, making them hard to detect or stealthy. Super-cruise is made possible by advanced engine designs that greatly enhance both the range and endurance of the platform, which in turn expands the roles, tasks, and missions' matrix. Future platforms are being designed to make extensive use of AI, incorporate MUMT ability to control unmanned wingmen and swarms, Electronic Warfare (EW)-resistant fibre optics, advanced photonics to replace electronics, greatly enhanced data acquisition and control, internal power generation for laser and hypersonic weapons, modular system suites for easy maintenance and upgrade options, and advanced engines capable of efficient operation across the entire range of subsonic operations to potentially hypersonic speeds in the future. Most importantly, they will have to be adept at penetrating deep into highly contested battlespaces of the future and undertake a wide range of missions. The list of future-relevant design requirements is likely to keep increasing with the rapidly growing needs of future warfighting.[36,37] The key focus areas for future aviation-related technological developments will, therefore, necessitate extensive and seamless hand-holding between military aviation practitioners, R&D specialists, and the defence industry.

The critical concern is that the already delayed Advanced Medium Combat Aircraft (AMCA) project is expected to take a decade before the platforms can be inducted into service, by which time China would be able to alter the air power balance in the region in its favour. This effectively means that by the time the 5th generation AMCA arrives, so would China's 6th generation platform, effectively continuing to leave India well behind the curve. Of equal concern is that in this period, IAF's mainstay 4th generation fleet will have also become a decade older, despite their upgraded capabilities. This does not bode well from a larger strategic perspective as Beijing's increasing leveraging of its air power capabilities as an instrument of its coercive foreign policy over Taiwan, and the East and South China Seas, are a harbinger of their future employment against India. The already visible increase in PLAAF's air activity across the disputed borders has made the territorial border issue more complex with the inclusion of the sanctity and security of India's sovereign air space. After building extensive infrastructure across the disputed regions, which includes the creation of border villages, an increase in aerial violations and coercive air activity in both Ladakh and Arunachal Pradesh can be expected as the new normal, to bolster Beijing's narrative building to support its territorial ambitions.

Thus, to ride the turbulent times ahead, the urgent fulfilment of the Multi-Role Fighter Aircraft (MRFA) requirement to bolster India's 4.5 generation inventory of its medium-weight category of fighters is not just an IAF requirement but indeed a national security imperative. Two squadrons of Rafale are nowhere enough, and the urgent necessity of bolstering the 4.5 generation capability cannot be overemphasised. This is because the upgraded MiG 29, Mirage 2000 and Jaguar fleets would reach obsolescence and will need replacement well before the AMCA squadrons become operational. This will gravely and irretrievably impact IAF in both quantum and quality, as even with the best possible bolstering of indigenous production capacity over the coming years, it will not be possible to arrest any further decline of India's combat air power capabilities.

The Tejas Mk 1A program is behind schedule as the first rollout has slipped from 31 Mar 2024 to Nov 2024. The long history of deadline slippages over the years, along with the MRFA imbroglio, has adversely affected IAF's combat status and led to an irreversible downturn in its combat inventory. The improved Mk 1A production with updated avionics, an active electronically scanned array radar, and an updated EW suite is pretty much at the mercy of the US General Electrics, which was to supply the F404 engines in financial year 2023-24 and has not yet done so. Similarly, despite its impressive, planned capabilities, the projected production timelines of the Tejas Mk 2 in the desired numbers depend on the Indian Aeronautical Development Agency's capacity to produce the F414 engines in the required numbers.[38] To complicate matters the Hindustan Aeronautics Limited (HAL) has recently confirmed a delay in supply of the F414 engine, and will now delay the Tejas Mk 2 as well. The order book of HAL remains the envy of India's defence industry, standing at INR 94,000 cr at the end of the financial year 2023-24. That is more than three times the company's turnover of INR 29,810 cr last year, and yet, the harsh reality of its actual production capability is causing serious degradation in the nation's air power capacity.[39]

India's *Atmanirbharta* (Self-reliance) strategy is a national imperative to foster much-needed self-reliance, especially in the defence sector, and conceptually, this is certainly the way forward. While many initiatives are underway towards indigenisation, an inescapable reality is that *Atmanirbharta* in fighter development and achieving the necessary scale of fighter production is a long-term strategy. There is no doubt the R&D and production capacity need generous investment; indeed, it will take well over a decade for *Atmanirbharta* to become truly indigenous. Thus, given this stark reality, there is no choice but to pursue foreign purchases over the next decade to prevent an irrecoverable gap in combat capability and capacity within India's fighter fleet, which must be taken seriously and urgently by the national leadership and policymakers.

Therefore, considering the long timelines fighter programs take to mature and reach the desired levels of production rate, limiting the AMCA program to 5th generation design requirements would be a strategic mistake. With no industry benchmarks on what exactly constitutes a 6th generation fighter, the AMCA development must, therefore, include truly new-generation capabilities. Though easier said than done, India's fighter production industry and ecosystem need not only generous budgetary support, but also an aggressive and innovative strategy to accelerate development and enhance production capacity, with stringent accountability and governmental oversight.

The harsh fact is that the IAF's declining numbers of combat platforms has created an ever increasing inventory gap due to an inadequate future 'Fill Rate' and is already in a downward spiral. Future inductions will no longer be able to close the gap fill until we achieve a serious production capacity. In the face of the serious strategic consequences of an inevitable and continued further decline in our combat capability, in the interim, direct foreign purchase of the 114 MRFA is inescapable reality, for which the Government has to bite the bullet. Despite past controversies and concerns, a bilateral partnership for additional joint-produced Rafales in India makes strategic sense, with an attendant long-term agreement for joint upgrades and technology transfer access on future 4.5 generation plus variants of the platform and its weapons suite. It will enable a steady and stable induction from a reliable partner, ensure greater platform commonality, assure future platform and weapons upgrades, and future engine development for the AMCA. It will enable a future relevant strategic balancing of the IAF's Russia-centric dependency of its inventory basket to include another reliable partner nation and obviate any dependency on a temperamental US military industry while fostering Indian defence production. Considering India's current foreign policy standing, this is an imperative which needs to be fast-tracked.

CHAPTER 8

Aerospace Technology and Production Capability

"IAF aims to create an ecosystem which fosters innovation and encourages technology development in Defence by engaging R&D institutes, academia, industries, start-ups, and even individual innovators".

- Air Chief Marshal VR Chaudhari[40]

The rapidly changing operational environment entails that the IAF can no longer afford to develop aerospace systems on the traditional linear acquisition and development timelines. Increasing the capability development pace is critical to narrowing and closing the gap against an adversary whose pace and capacity in the aerospace field is way ahead of us. There is no option but for the Indian aerospace industry to evolve swiftly so that capability development remains relevant. The aerospace technology and production have to become adaptable, affordable and agile to stay ahead of the curve of future aerospace power needs. In the immediate near-term, maximise collaborative R&D in science and technology, between the academia, industry and the military. Simultaneously bring in agile acquisition processes and time-sensitive acquisition policies which shrinks the development-production-operationalisation lag. Continuing with the traditional approaches will result in a fatal technology gap in India's critical warfighting capabilities vis-à-vis the technologically superior adversary. 'Digital engineering must be leveraged to ensure smart commonality and interoperability across all fleets and systems across all services wherever possible—common support equipment, common system configurations, common interfaces, common architecture, even common components—that simplify the logistics and maintenance in the field'.[41]

The pace of technological advancements can only increase if the IAF and the industry synergistically short-circuit the synapses between the development of future operational concepts, identifying operational requirements, industrial research, development and production and finally, operational testing and evaluation. This should be addressed on the highest priority, given the long distance and lead times between the drawing board and the field.

India must vigorously expand its aviation and weapon technology-related education, R&D base, by leveraging the nation's large tech-savvy youth population. The military aviation industry in Asia and especially the global south has immense growth and expansion potential, providing it with a strategic opportunity to take the lead. It will make the *Atmanirbharta* a robust long-term strategic reality that it needs to become, and it will also expand India's defence export base and add the desirable advantage of creating a regional strategic dependency.

Civil aviation along with the IAF and aviation elements of the other services constitute the nation's CAP, and the nation must realise the immense potential of the defence and civil aviation industry. There are vast areas of overlap between civil and military aviation in national security due to interoperability of capabilities, and capacity redundancies. It also has enormous untapped potential to contribute to economic growth, foreign policy support, diplomacy, political support and signalling, humanitarian assistance, and more, with certainly even more to offer in the future. A new approach is needed that embraces public-private partnerships and invests heavily to flip it into a profit-making economic venture. India's aviation industry expects INR 35,000 cr (USD 4.99 bn) investment in the next four years, as the government plans to invest USD 1.83 bn for the development of airport infrastructure and aviation navigation services, and build 220 new airports by 2025.[42] India is already known for cost-competitive space research, development and production. Expanding this model to an integrated military-civil aviation industry will be a truly strategic investment for the future, given the immense regional demand for affordable combat platforms, critical enablers, AD radars, weapon systems, aerial weapons, fixed and rotary-wing civilian passenger and transport aircraft, unmanned platforms, etc. The list of possibilities is endless. It will not only fill our inventory gaps, but generating extensive low-cost competitive exports will also expand our regional influence by creating technology dependencies.

Given the continued future strategic significance of the security-contested IOR for India, the rapidly evolving security construct of the Indo-Pacific, and the existing continental threat dynamics, the nation needs an air strategy and an air advisor for the future requirements of a comprehensive national air power capability from a security perspective. The growth trajectory of the civil aviation industry and the future developmental requirements of India's immense aerospace industry potential, the need for synergising India's future military and civil aviation needs make these two an imperative. In its continued absence, the nation will be bereft of professional inputs on an important instrument of a multi-domain full spectrum military power but also marginalise the nation's immense future CAP necessity.

To its advantage, India has a strategic window of opportunity to create an ecosystem of cooperative development and production with regional partners. This will enhance India's regional stature as a significant defence industry partner and foster greater regional air power interoperability, contributing to multi-domain influence, and strategic dependency amongst key regional nations.

The need for a comprehensive approach to synergise India's military aviation, civil aviation, and defence-space necessities of the future, in sync with the nation's future security needs, growth and long-term interests, necessitates the creation of the position of a national air and space advisor in the national security establishment. This will set the pace for greater development of India's enormous potential in the aviation industry and future leveraging of the nation's air power.

Conclusion

"Hence, even as the relative equation of power among nations changes due to the global power shifts from the West to the East as a consequence of the rise of China and India, there is more rather than less to suggest that aerospace power has become the military instrument of choice in an uncertain world".[43]

- *Jasjit Singh*

Ongoing wars and conflicts are influenced by the political dynamics and national interests of those involved. With attention often focused on immediate goals, there's a risk of drawing premature or incorrect conclusions. A critical contextual difference for India, unlike in recent conflicts, is the serious threat posed by adversarial air power in its future. Operational and tactical insights from current conflicts are still evolving, but strategic inferences concerning air power are clear and highly relevant to India's long-term military and security interests. These inferences will offer benchmarks for future air and space power development and underpin essential organisational, doctrinal, and employment strategies. Significantly, they represent areas for sustained strategic investment, aligning with India's goals for a self-reliant aerospace defence industry, critical to addressing its future security needs.

The extensive use of air power in current wars and conflicts highlights its continued relevance, supported by expanding methods of deployment—manned and unmanned platforms, diverse long-range precision weapons, hypersonic and advanced aerial missiles, sophisticated air defence systems, as well as surface and space-launched weapons that operate across the aerospace continuum. Future non-kinetic capabilities leveraging the air and space domains further reinforce its enduring significance. Air power has become the essential, integrating thread in multi-domain operations, seamlessly connecting land, sea, and space. In addition to its role in national security, the aviation industry's vast growth potential represents an area India must strategically invest in, serving the broader national interest. Over the coming decades, India's *Atmanirbharta* strategy will require dedicated investment and nurturing as a long-term path to self-reliance in both military and civil aviation sectors. This approach promises substantial benefits for national defence autonomy and economic growth. However, during the development phase, until India's defence sector reaches the desired innovation and production capability, national security will realistically rely on critical foreign procurements aligned with future-relevant strategic partnerships.

Air and space power are two domains with vast unrealised potential. Effective deterrence is fundamentally grounded in a nation's offensive military capabilities, where the future possibilities of air and space realms are significant. China remains resolute in its pursuit of becoming a world-class military power by 2047, an ambition aimed at asserting its role as the central global state, or *Zhōngguó*. Aggressively focused on advancing its air and space power capabilities, China seeks to challenge the dominant US military presence. Meanwhile, India's growing economic and great-power status places it in strategic competition with China, particularly given unresolved border disputes and China's associated territorial claims. India's asymmetrical advantage in air power is essential to its conventional deterrence and a critical factor in future conflicts. Maintaining and leveraging this edge in the aerial domain will be decisive in shaping outcomes across potential wars and military contingencies.

Endnotes

1 Qiao Liang and Wang Xiangsui, 'Unrestricted Warfare', PLA Literature and Arts Publishing House, Beijing, Feb 1999, p. 36, Accessed on 20 Sep 2024

2 Ben Lewis, '2022 ADIZ Violations: China Dials Up Pressure on Taiwan', China Power, CSIS, 23 Mar 2023, Accessed on 20 Sep 2024, https://chinapower.csis.org/analysis/2022-adiz-violations-china-dials-up-pressure-on-taiwan/

3 Air Marshal (Dr) Diptendu Choudhury, 'Aerospace Power: IAF's Doctrinal Overview', ORF, 10 Feb 2023, Accessed on 20 Sep 2024, https://www.orfonline.org/expert-speak/aerospace-power-iafs-doctrinal-overview

4 Air Marshal (Dr) Diptendu Choudhury, 'Chariots of Fire', Medals and Ribbons, Apr-Jun 2024, Vol.4, Issue 2, Accessed on 20 Sep 2024, https://medalsandribbons.com/2024/03/23/chariots-of-fire/

5 Air Marshal (Dr) Diptendu Choudhury, 'A Waning Conventional Deterrence- A National Security Portent', VIF India, 22 Sep 2023, Accessed on 20 Sep 2024, https://www.vifindia.org/article/2023/september/22/A-Waning-Conventional-Deterrence-A-National-Security-Portent%20%20

6 Air Marshal (Dr) Diptendu Choudhury, 'Chariots of Fire', Medals and Ribbons, Apr-Jun 2024, Vol.4, Issue 2, Accessed on 20 Sep 2024, https://medalsandribbons.com/2024/03/23/chariots-of-fire/

7 Sanu Kainikara, 'The Cassandra Effect: Future Perceptions of Air Power', Vij Books India Pvt Ltd, New Delhi, 2016, p. 13, Accessed on 20 Sep 2024

8 Air Marshal (Dr) Diptendu Choudhury, 'Russia's Military Understanding of Air Power: Structural & Doctrinal Aspects', VIF India, 23 May 2022, Accessed on 25 Sep 2024, https://www.vifindia.org/article/2022/may/23/russia-s-military-understanding-of-air-power

Endnotes

9 Phillips Payson O'Brien and Edward Stringer, 'The Overlooked Reason Russia's Invasion Is Floundering', The Atlantic, 9 May 2022, Accessed on 25 Sep 2024, https://www.theatlantic.com/ideas/archive/2022/05/russian-military-air-force-failure-ukraine/629803/

10 Becca Wasser, Stacie L. Pettyjohn, Jeffrey Martini, Alexandra T. Evans, Karl P. Mueller, Nathaniel Edenfield, Gabrielle Tarini, Ryan Haberman, Jalen Zeman, 'The Role of Air Power in Defeating ISIS', Research Brief RAND Corporation, 12 Feb 2021, Accessed on 02 Oct 2024, https://www.rand.org/pubs/research_briefs/RBA388-1.html

11 Michael Simpson, Adam R. Grissom, Christopher A. Mouton, John P. Godges, Russell Hanson, 'Road to Damascus, The Russian Air Campaign in Syria 2015-2018', Research Report, RAND Corporation, 11 May 2022, Accessed on 02 Oct 2024, https://www.rand.org/pubs/research_reports/RRA11701.html#:~:text=Russian%20airpower%20played%20a%20decisive,power%20supporting%20regime%20ground%20forces

12 Air Marshal (Dr) Diptendu Choudhury, 'The Enduring Relevance of Offensive Air Power' in 'Force in Statecraft—An Indian Perspective', Ed Arjun Subramaniam and Diptendu Choudhury, KW Publishers, New Delhi, 2022, p. 208, Accessed on 02 Oct 2024

13 Air Marshal (Dr) Diptendu Choudhury, 'Chariots of Fire: Air War in Ukraine and Gaza- Takeaways for India', Medals and Ribbons, Apr-Jun 2024, Vol.4, Issue 2, Accessed on 11 Oct 2024, https://medalsandribbons.com/author/air-marshal-dr-diptendu-choudhury-pvsm-avsm-vm-vsm-retd/

14 Rosita Mickeviciute, 'Top 10 World's Best Military Drones in 2024 and Their Capabilities', Aerotime, 30 January 2024, Accessed on 11 Oct 2024, https://www.aerotime.aero/articles/25712-worlds-best-military-drones.

15 Thibault Spirlet, 'Tanks and Troops Out in the Open in Ukraine Can't Go 10 Minutes Without Being Spotted and Fired Upon, Ukrainian Official Says', Business Insider India, 29 Sep 2023, Accessed on 11 Oct 2024, https://www.businessinsider.com/tanks-troops-in-the-open-are-hit-within-10-minutes-ukraine-official-2023-9?r=USandIR=T

16 Air Commodore Jasjit Singh, 'Defence from the Skies', KW Publishers, New Delhi, 2012, p. 15, Accessed on 14 Oct 2024

17   Ukraine's Energy System Under Attack', IEA, Accessed on 14 Oct 2024   https://www.iea.org/reports/ukraines-energy-security-and-the-coming-winter/ukraines-energy-system-under-attack

18   Aura Sabadus, 'Russia's New Air Offensive Leaves Ukraine Facing Humanitarian Disaster', Atlantic Council, 31 Mar 2024, Accessed on 14 Oct 2024, https://www.atlanticcouncil.org/blogs/ukrainealert/russias-new-air-offensive-leaves-ukraine-facing-humanitarian-disaster/

19   'Global Air Powers Ranking', WDMMA, 2024, Accessed on 14 Oct 2024 https://www.wdmma.org/ranking.php

20   General MM Naravane, 'Air Space Management: Need For Review', Indian Aerospace and Defence Bulletin, 11 Feb 2023, Accessed on 22 Oct 2024, https://www.iadb.in/2023/02/11/air-space-management-need-for-review/

21   Air Marshal (Dr) Diptendu Choudhury, 'Air Defence is Everywhere', VIF India, 24 Jul 2020, Accessed on 22 Oct 2024, https://www.vifindia.org/article/2020/july/24/air-defence-is-everywhere

22   'India Prepares For 'One Airspace': Unified Air Traffic Control Plans Set in Motion – What It Means', Times of India, 6 Apr 2024, Accessed on 23 Oct 2024, https://timesofindia.indiatimes.com/business/india-business/india-prepares-for-one-airspace-unified-air-traffic-control-plans-set-in-motion-what-it-means/articleshow/109084063.cms

23   'Pakistan Suffers Over Rs 8 bn in Losses Due to Airspace Closure', PTI, 19 Jul 2019, Accessed on 23 Oct 2024, https://economictimes.indiatimes.com/news/international/business/pakistan-suffers-over-8-billion-in-losses-due-to-airspace-closure/articleshow/70290104.cms?from=mdr

24   Airports Authority of India, 'Manual on Flexible Use of Airspace – India, Version 1.0', International Civil Aviation Organisation, 3 Apr 2015, Accessed on 24 Oct 2024, https://www.icao.int/APAC/Meetings/2015%20ATFM_SG5/WP13%20Manual%20on%20Flexible%20Use%20of%20Airspace%20-%20India.pdf

25   Joelle Charbonneau, 'From A to Z: A Lesson in Air Defence Identification Zones and Depoliticizing Airspace', Asia Pacific Foundation of Canada, 7 Sep 2016, Accessed on 24 Oct 2024, https://www.asiapacific.ca/blog/z-lesson-air-defence-identification-zones-and-depoliticizing

Endnotes

26   Air Marshal (Dr) Diptendu Choudhury, 'Air Defence is Everywhere', VIF India, 24 Jul 2020, Accessed on 24 Oct 2024, https://www.vifindia.org/article/2020/july/24/air-defence-is-everywhere.

27   'Space will Cast its Influence on Air, Maritime, And Land Domains: CDS', PTI, 18 Apr 2024, Accessed on 24 Oct 2024 https://economictimes.indiatimes.com/news/defence/space-will-cast-its-influence-on-air-maritime-and-land-domains-chief-of-defence-staff/articleshow/109396186.cms?from=mdr

28   Anthony H. Cordesman, 'Chinese Space Strategy and Developments', Center for Strategic and International Studies, 19 Aug 2016, Accessed on 24 Oct 2024, https://www.csis.org/analysis/china-space-strategy-and-developments

29   'Karman Line', Britannica, Accessed on 24 Oct 2024 https://www.britannica.com/science/Karman-line

30   Air Marshal (Dr) Diptendu Choudhury , 'The IAF's Transformation into the Indian Air and Space Force', Chanakya Forum, 25 Jan 2024, Accessed on 24 Oct 2024, https://chanakyaforum.com/the-iafs-transformation-into-the-indian-air-and-space-force/

31   'Doctrine of the Indian Air Force', IAP 2000-22, Accessed on 25 Oct 2024, https://indianairforce.nic.in/wp-content/uploads/2023/01/2MB.pdf

32   Air Marshal (Dr) Diptendu Choudhury, 'Hellfire from the Heavens: A Perspective on Contemporary Aerial Strikes', VIF, 4 Jun 2024, Accessed on 25 Oct 2024, https://www.vifindia.org/article/2024/june/04/Hellfire-from-the-Heavens-A-Perspective-on-Contemporary-Aerial-Strikes

33   Air Marshal (Dr) Diptendu Choudhury , 'The IAF's Transformation into the Indian Air and Space Force', Chanakya Forum, 25 Jan 2024, Accessed on 25 Oct 2024, https://chanakyaforum.com/the-iafs-transformation-into-the-indian-air-and-space-force/

34   Ibid

35   ACM Arup Raha, 'Squadron Strength: Measure of Air Power', The Chanakya Diaries, Inaugural Issue, Monsoon 2024, p. 35, Accessed on 26 Oct 2024

36   Maxwell Goldstein, 'Sixth Generation Fighter Programs', Grey Dynamics, 01 Feb 2024, Accessed on 26 Oct 2024, https://greydynamics.com/sixth-generation-fighter-programs/

37 Joseph Noronha, 'Sixth Generation Fighters: Closer Than You Think', Aero India Special Edition, 2021, Accessed on 26 Oct 2024, https://www.sps-aviation.com/story/?id=2884andh=6th-Generation-Fighters-Closer-Than-You-Think

38 'Indian ADA to Roll Tejas Mark II Prototype With F-414 Engine by 2024 End', Hindustan Times, 21 Jun 2023, Accessed on 28 Oct 2024, https://www.hindustantimes.com/india-news/indian-ada-to-roll-tejas-mark-ii-prototype-with-f-414-engine-by-2024-end-101687323394817.html

39 'The Tejas Mark 2 Challenge: Advanced Upgrades for Superior Air Power', 30 May 2024, Accessed on 29 Oct 2024, https://www.business-standard.com/external-affairs-defence-security/news/the-tejas-mark-2-challenge-building-a-more-powerful-capable-fighter-124052901703_1.html

40 Kamal Shah, 'IAF Chief Details Aerospace Advancements & Vision For Self-Reliant Future', Indian Aerospace and Defence Bulletin, 2 Oct 2023, Accessed on 29 Oct 2024, https://www.iadb.in/2023/10/02/iaf-chief-details-aerospace-advancements-vision-for-self-reliant-future/

41 Dr Will Roper, 'Take the Red Pill: The New Digital Acquisition Reality', Cited by Valerie Insinna, Defense News, 15 Sep 2020, Accessed on 29 Oct 2024, https://www.defensenews.com/breaking-news/2020/09/15/the-us-air-force-has-built-and-flown-a-mysterious-full-scale-prototype-of-its-future-fighter-jet/

42 Aviation Industry Report Jun 2022, Accessed on 22 Oct 2024, https://www.ibef.org/industry/indian-aviation#:~:text=Market%20Size,airplanes%20operating%20in%20the%20sector

43 Air Commodore Jasjit Singh, 'Defence from the Skies', KW Publishers, New Delhi, 2012, p. 285, Accessed on 22 Oct 2024